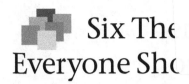 

Six Themes
Everyone Should Know

Philippians

Cynthia M. Campbell

Geneva
Press

© 2020 Geneva Press

First edition
Published by Geneva Press
Louisville, Kentucky

20 21 22 23 24 25 26 27 28—10 9 8 7 6 5 4 3 2 1

Unless otherwise indicated, Scripture quotations are from the New Revised Standard Version of the Bible, © 1989 by the Division of Christian Education of the National Council of the Churches of Christ in the U.S.A., and used by permission. In some instances, adaptations have been made to a Scripture or a confession to make the language inclusive.

Excerpts from the *Book of Order* and *Book of Confessions* have been used throughout this resource. Both are reprinted with permission of the Office of the General Assembly.

Cover designer: Rebecca Kueber

Library of Congress Cataloging-in-Publication Data

Names: Campbell, Cynthia McCall, author. | Stimson, Eva.
Title: Philippians / Cynthia M. Campbell.
Description: First edition. | Louisville, Kentucky: Geneva Press, [2020] |
    Series: Six themes everyone should know
Identifiers: LCCN 2020000132 (print) | LCCN 2020000133 (ebook) | ISBN
    9781571532411 (paperback) | ISBN 9781611649925 (ebook)
Subjects: LCSH: Bible. Philippians--Theology.
Classification: LCC BS2705.52 .C35 2020 (print) | LCC BS2705.52 (ebook) |
    DDC 227/.606--dc23
LC record available at https://lccn.loc.gov/2020000132
LC ebook record available at https://lccn.loc.gov/2020000133

Most Geneva Press books are available at special quantity discounts when purchased in bulk by corporations, organizations, and special-interest groups. For more information, please e-mail SpecialSales@GenevaPress.com.

Contents

Six Themes Everyone Should Know series

Introduction to the
Six Themes Everyone Should Know series

The *Six Themes Everyone Should Know* series focuses on the study of Scripture. Bible study is vital to the lives of churches. Churches need ways of studying Scripture that can fit a variety of contexts and group needs. *Six Themes Everyone Should Know* studies offer a central feature of church adult educational programs. Their flexibility and accessibility make it possible to have short-term studies that introduce biblical books and their main themes.

Six Themes Everyone Should Know consists of six chapters that introduce major biblical themes. At the core of each chapter is an introduction and three major sections. These sections relate to key dimensions of Bible study. These sections ask:

- What does this biblical theme mean?
- What is the meaning of this biblical theme for the life of faith?
- What does this biblical theme mean for the church at this point in history for action?

This format presents a compact and accessible way for people in various educational settings to gain knowledge about major themes in the biblical books; to experience the impact of what Scripture means for Christian devotion to God; and to consider ways Scripture can lead to new directions for the church in action.

Introduction to *Philippians*

Philippians is one of the most winsome of all of Paul's letters, and it provides an amazingly intimate view of the early church. It is largely free of the conflicts so evident in Paul's letters to the Galatians and Corinthians. In fact, Philippians is often called the "epistle of joy" because of the warmth with which Paul expresses himself toward his friends. There is a poignancy to Paul's joy, however, because he is in prison and does not know whether he will be set free or put to death.

In his very helpful commentary, noted preacher and New Testament scholar Fred Craddock introduces this letter by saying that it is "a letter from Paul to a church."[1] First of all, this is a *letter* that was intended to be read aloud in worship—not as "scripture" but as a pastoral communication from this community's founder to his dear friends. Paul uses the form or structure of letter writing that was common in his day. First, there is a greeting or salutation (1:1-2). This is followed by words of thanksgiving (vv. 3-11) in which Paul celebrates the ties that bind him to this congregation. The body of this letter (1:12-3:1) is a combination of theological reflection and discussion of his own situation. The letter continues with moral or ethical instruction (3:1b-4:9). Again according to the tradition of letter writing of the time, Paul concludes with final words, personal greetings, and a closing blessing or benediction (4:10-23).

Second, this is a letter *from Paul*. Scholars debate whether some writings in the New Testament that carry Paul's name were actually written by him (e.g., Colossians and 1 and 2 Timothy). But about Philippians there is no debate. The only question is: when did he write this letter? Paul tells us that he is in prison and mentions the "imperial guard" (1:13), but otherwise there is no internal evidence for where he might be. According to Acts, Paul was in prison several times, but there is no clear way to connect those incidents with this letter. Some argue that this was written

1. Fred B. Craddock, *Philippians*, Interpretation: A Bible Commentary for Teaching and Preaching (Louisville, KY: Westminster John Knox Press, 2012), 2.

near the end of Paul's life (the early 60s) when he was in prison in Rome (where he would be put to death). Others suggest that the letter was written earlier, when he was in prison in Ephesus (in the early 50s) or Caesarea (the late 50s). These earlier dates seem more plausible because of the references to the travel back and forth of his friend Epaphroditus. The specifics matter less than that Paul is writing to reassure his friends in Philippi that, even though his own fate is uncertain, he is confident that the power of God is present with him as it is with them.

Finally, this is a letter to *a church*. Between the letter and the story of Paul's arrival in Philippi in Acts 16, we probably know more about this community of faith than any other that Paul founded. In Acts, we read about Lydia, the first to be baptized and the first to extend hospitality to Paul and his companions. There is good reason to think that she will emerge as one of the first leaders of this community. But we know about others as well: Epaphroditus (whom the Philippians have sent to help Paul during his imprisonment), Euodia, Syntyche, and Clement. All of these are named as "co-workers" or colleagues. Euodia and Syntyche are women, signaling that a time of shared leadership between women and men existed in the early days of the Christian movement. Finally, we see evidence that Paul has maintained close ties to the Philippians in the years since his departure. At the end of the letter, he thanks them for their financial as well as spiritual support as he continued on his journey.

There are many wonderful themes to explore in this letter, but fundamentally it invites us to reflect on the nature of Christian community and the nature of the communities of faith in which we find ourselves. In a society that values individualism and tends to see spirituality as a personal and private matter, this letter is a strong corrective as it shows the strong bonds of friendship and support that come from being united to one another through Jesus Christ.

For all the variations in Christian faith and practice (both ancient and modern), Christianity without community is simply not Christian.

Chapter 1

In This Together

Scripture
Philippians 1:3–7; Acts 16:11–15, 40   Being in relationship or partnership with others is at the heart of Christian faith and experience. This chapter invites us to recommit ourselves to the practice of Christian community.

Prayer
Dear God, in Jesus Christ, you make us one with each other and with you. Help us to seek and find you in our communities of faith so that we may live as witnesses to your love for all. Amen.

Introduction
Where do you come from? Many of us are trying to trace our ancestry. We look for clues to our own identity in the stories of those who have gone before us. The Bible is the great storybook for Jews and Christians. It is where we go to discover our ancestors in faith and to discern how we are to follow God in the present. Paul's letter to the community in Philippi is one window into our beginnings as Christians. Between the account of Paul's visit in Acts 16 and the letter itself, we get a remarkably intimate picture of this community and the people who made it up.

Philippi was a city of some ten thousand people in what was then called Macedonia (now part of Greece). It was located on the

Via Egnatia, a major Roman road that connected Constantinople (now Istanbul) with Rome. Although the city's roots go back to the fifth century BCE, it was "re-founded" as a Roman colony in 31 BCE by Roman soldiers and their families following a major battle in the region. By the time Paul arrived, in approximately 49 CE, Philippi was a thriving city surrounded by an agricultural area. While both ethnically and culturally diverse, it was organized and governed by Roman law and custom.

Philippi is Paul's first destination outside Asia Minor, the first city he visited in Europe, and his first mission in a place where there was no Jewish community from which to begin preaching. While there are many discrepancies between events recounted in Paul's letters and the stories in Acts, most scholars agree that the portrayal of Paul's early days in Philippi in Acts 16 is fairly accurate.

When Paul and Silas arrive, they go to what is described as "a place of prayer" (Acts 16:13), because there evidently was no synagogue. There they meet Lydia, a merchant who was a dealer in purple cloth. She and her household are Paul's first audience and first converts. Evidently a woman of significant means, Lydia invites Paul and Silas to make her home their base of operations. Thus begins the church in Philippi.

A Basic Theme: *Koinonia*

The Greek word *koinonia* figures prominently in Paul's Letter to the Philippians. Some congregations today use the word *koinonia* to describe small-group ministries of various kinds. It is often translated "fellowship," a term that conjures up potluck suppers and progressive dinners—activities designed to build relationships among church members. Some find these enjoyable; others avoid them.

Koinonia appears at the very beginning of Paul's letter (1:5). The NRSV translates it as "sharing," while the Common English Bible uses "partners." It can also be translated "communion" and "participation." All these terms imply mutuality. People involved in a koinonia relationship are engaged together with a common purpose. They work alongside one another toward a shared goal. They exercise a shared responsibility for one another in endeavors that bind them together. The concept of koinonia implies relationships built up over time that create community and communion.

Paul's life work was the founding and nurturing of Christian communities. Paul was a tireless traveler as he shared the good news of Jesus Christ. Often it seems that Paul was a "lone ranger" of sorts, a towering figure of great intellect and deep wisdom. But it is also clear that this founder of communities exercised his ministry in partnership with others. Nowhere is that more evident than in Philippi. We know who Paul's partners were, and a significant number of them were women.

First of all, there is Lydia. She is the first convert in Philippi. She opened her home to Paul and his companions, and by the time they left the city, it had become the locus of the new Christian community (see Acts 16:40). It is widely thought by scholars that the one in whose home the community gathered was the leader of that community. It is not unreasonable to assume that, after Paul left Philippi, Lydia became the overseer or one of the "bishops" whom Paul greets in Philippians 1:1.

In chapter 4, Paul mentions two other leaders, Euodia and Syntyche (4:2–3). It appears that they are involved in some sort of disagreement, and Paul urges another, unnamed leader to help them resolve their differences. The important thing, however, is that these two women are named as "co-workers" who have "struggled beside" Paul in building up the community.

Paul also refers to two other leaders, Timothy and Epaphroditus (2:19–30). It appears that Epaphroditus was a member of the Philippian community who had left with Paul and whom now Paul was sending back, perhaps carrying this letter. Paul also hopes to send Timothy, his young protégé, whom he trusts will provide the leadership and care Paul knows they need.

Koinonia (partnership) in the gospel is one of the themes of this letter, and what the letter shows is partnership in action.

The Life of Faith: Partners in Ministry

From the very beginning, following Jesus meant being in community. One of the first things Jesus did was to invite Simon, Andrew, James, and John to become his disciples, his students. Over time, the group grew to include the Twelve and Mary Magdalene, as well as other women, who provided financial support for the mission (Luke 8:2–3). According to Acts, this larger group of followers made Jerusalem their headquarters after the resurrection.

They told the story of Jesus, baptized those who wanted to join them, and created a new community. They continued to pray in the temple, broke bread together (probably both a meal and what would become the Lord's Supper), and cared for one another both financially and spiritually.

Wherever he went, Paul (following the pattern of other evangelists before him) founded communities and tried to teach them what Christian community meant. As we will see in chapters 3 and 4, Paul's understanding of Christian community depends entirely on how he understands the death and resurrection of Jesus Christ. That pattern is what sets the tone, in Paul's mind, for the life of the church. For now, the important thing to recognize is that Christian faith is faith lived out in community with others. As far as Paul is concerned, being a disciple of Jesus is not a solitary journey or a simply personal quest. To be with Jesus is to become deeply related to others and to live with one another in deep communion.

Within the community, some are designated as leaders, people with particular responsibilities for the well-being of the group. While we don't know enough to see a particular polity (or form of church order) emerging, what we do see is that ministry is never a solo venture. Just as Paul did not work alone, so he wants to make sure that the churches he has founded understand that working together is necessary. Paul calls these other leaders "co-workers"; he says that they "struggle" together toward the common goal of sharing the gospel. It is not too much to say that this mutuality in ministry is a direct outgrowth of the gospel itself.

Perhaps the most intriguing discovery in a close reading of Philippians is how many of these leaders were women. When we think about Paul and the question of women's leadership, our images are almost entirely negative. For centuries, the church has quoted 1 Corinthians 14:33b–36 ("women should be silent in the churches") as though that was the last word on the subject. Philippians paints a far different picture. Not only are there women in leadership, but we also know their names! We know that the movement itself depended on them (as the community under Lydia's leadership depended on the hospitality of her home). We see how important it was that these women coworkers be in substantial agreement about the church's mission and practices. Of all the biblical grounds for the ordination of women to the ministries of the church, Paul's testimony in this letter is the strongest. Other, more restrictive passages should be read in light of Philippians, and not the other way around.

The Church: Embracing Common Life

We live in a culture in which community is increasingly optional and an option that many people no longer seem to desire. Fewer people are joining traditional service organizations. It is often difficult to recruit for the PTA. Fewer people are active in a political party. Some years ago, sociologist Robert Putnam wrote that surveys suggested that, while more people are bowling, fewer are joining bowling leagues. They prefer "bowling alone."[1]

This trend is particularly true with respect to faith. More and more people see faith as an individual journey or quest. They have come to distrust religious institutions and no longer see religious community as a necessary part of faith. For many, faith is not only an individual path of spiritual development; but also a path that each individual creates on her or his own, often drawing on the resources of a wide variety of religious traditions.

In some ways, this current way of seeing faith or spirituality is a logical outgrowth of the modern evangelical movement in the United States. Beginning with the first Great Awakening in the early eighteenth century, Protestant preachers began to put heavy emphasis on individual conversion and personal religious experience. What mattered was not, they said, adhering to orthodox beliefs or even living a moral life. What mattered was whether the individual had a deep personal conviction of sin and also a sense of God's redeeming grace in Jesus Christ. Faith became a personal and eventually private matter.

The New Testament presents a different picture. For all the variations in Christian faith and practice (both ancient and modern), Christianity without community is simply not Christian. Becoming a follower of Christ began with baptism in which the individual became united with Christ and a member of Christ's body, the church. Perhaps the most remarkable religious and ethical insight of Christian faith is that baptism creates a new community in which the boundaries that human beings create

1. Robert D. Putnam, *Bowling Alone: The Collapse and Revival of American Community* (New York: Simon & Schuster, 2000).

are washed away. Divisions based on race or ethnicity, social or economic status, and even gender no longer matter for those who are in Christ (see Galatians 3:28). All are now brothers and sisters, and the rule of the community is the love seen in Christ himself.

Community begins in congregations, but ideally it extends globally. The local church is at its best when it is a community of care and challenge—when people have the opportunity to give and receive support from one another and when all are challenged to grow in faith and discipleship. But Christian community is not intended to be limited to small groups. When we affirm that we believe in the "catholic church," we mean that all followers of Christ, from every nation and culture, are members with one another of the one body of Christ. Modern denominational barriers make this difficult to see, but Christian unity remains a goal to which all of us are called.

Spiritual Practice

If your congregation has a prayer list in the bulletin or on a website, pray for those members by name. If you use the Presbyterian Church (U.S.A.)'s *Book of Common Worship*, you will find that the intercessions in morning and evening prayer suggest parts of the world and different denominational families each day for prayer.

For Reflection and Action

1. What faith communities have nurtured you? Who are some of the people who helped you learn the faith?

2. How do the people in the congregation of which you are a part support one another? How does your congregation challenge you to deeper discipleship?

3. What do you think of the claim that Christianity without community is not Christian?

The joy that Paul is talking about is an emotion and something far deeper than emotion. It is a way of looking at reality; it is a stance toward the world; it is a lens through which to see beneath the surface to deeper truth.

Chapter 2

Great Joy

Scripture
Philippians 1:4, 12–19; 4:4–7   Although he is in prison when he writes this letter, Paul is full of joy. This chapter invites us to reflect on how the gospel brings joy even as we confront the brokenness of our world in the pain in our own lives.

Prayer
Dear God, you are the source of all that is good. Open our hearts to the beauty all around and within so that we may rejoice with you in the goodness of your creation, even in times of danger and distress; through Jesus Christ our Lord. Amen.

Introduction
The overwhelming themes of Paul's letter to the Christian community in Philippi are *joy* and *rejoice!* What is striking is the context in which Paul writes about his own deep and abiding joy: Paul is in prison. Some scholars argue that this imprisonment was in Rome, because of the mention of the "imperial guard" (the *praetorium*). If that is the case, then this letter was likely written near the end of Paul's life. Others point out that the term *praetorium* was used for any major Roman garrison. Thus, many argue that Paul's incarceration was in Ephesus (much nearer to Philippi), which

would suggest a much earlier date for the letter (perhaps in the early 50s, not too long after Paul left Philippi). The intimate tone of the letter and the number of individuals mentioned by name would seem to support the theory of an earlier composition date and nearby location.

By his own account, Paul clashed frequently with authorities and was imprisoned with some regularity. Acts 16 says that this happened in Philippi itself in the early days of Paul's ministry there. That incarceration seems to have been brief, but the one mentioned in Philippians is long enough for Paul to continue his work by writing to his friends. A number of modern counterparts come to mind. Dietrich Bonhoeffer's *Letters and Papers from Prison* and Martin Luther King's "Letter from a Birmingham Jail" are both examples of writings by pastors who were put in prison because of their work on behalf of peace and justice. Their writings are powerful testimonies of continuing ministry in the midst of danger.

What exactly was it about Paul and his preaching that was so dangerous and disruptive? To our modern ears, nothing in Paul's writing seems overtly political. Some answers may emerge as we read further into this letter. It will become clearer in chapter 3.

A Basic Theme: "Joyful, Joyful . . ."

The word "joy" (*chara*) and related words like "rejoice" are used fourteen times in this letter. The tone of the entire letter is set at the very beginning: "I thank my God every time I remember you, constantly praying *with joy* in every one of my prayers for all of you" (1:3–4). From the very beginning, Paul indicates the joy he feels as he thinks about this community of faith and the people with whom he has shared so much. There are doubtless deep, personal ties between them, but it seems that the joy that Paul describes goes beyond friendship. It is surely based on their shared faith and Paul's experience of seeing people's lives transformed by the power of the good news of Jesus Christ. As these men and women have found new meaning and hope in their lives, as they have become a community of care, as they have begun sharing their faith with others, Paul feels the deep and abiding joy of ministry bearing rich fruit.

The theme continues as Paul reflects on his imprisonment. "Yes, and I will continue to rejoice, for I know that through your prayers and the help of the Spirit of Jesus Christ this [imprisonment] will turn out for my deliverance" (1:18b–19). Clearly, Paul is trying to reassure his friends that he is not in immediate danger. But he is also trying to help them see that suffering may be part of following the gospel path and that it is not to be feared. His joy comes from knowing that he is being obedient to his calling and from the support he is confident he has from his Philippian friends. Paul can rejoice because of what they share with one another in Christ.

In one of the most familiar and widely used passages in this letter, Paul draws the theme of joy to its conclusion. Now he is not merely expressing his own faith and conviction. He is encouraging others to join him in this remarkable orientation toward life. "Rejoice in the Lord always; again I will say, Rejoice. Let your gentleness be known to everyone. The Lord is near. Do not worry about anything, but in everything by prayer and supplication with thanksgiving let your requests be made known to God. And the peace of God, which surpasses all understanding, will guard your hearts and your minds in Christ Jesus" (4:4–7).

Here Paul suggests that being joyful or rejoicing is a kind of spiritual discipline. If one can be exhorted to "rejoice," then the kind of joy Paul has in mind is more than the feeling of enjoyment that comes from something pleasurable. The kind of joy that Paul has and wants for his friends is a mind-set, a way of looking at reality and one's experience. Because God is good and gracious, we can be confident regardless of the outward circumstances of our lives. Because God can be trusted to be with us and for us, we know that tragedy, loss, danger, and death will never have the last word. Knowing that is cause to rejoice!

The Life of Faith: The Meaning of Joy

One of the more unfortunate features of modern life is a pervasive skepticism that often bleeds over into cynicism. We are increasingly distrustful of institutions—including the church—that once commanded widespread respect. Because scams come at us through various forms of media, we are taught to be cautious. We know that if something looks too good to be true, it probably is. Modern life requires a considerable amount of critical thinking, but when that becomes cynicism, it makes comprehending Paul's emphasis on joy very difficult. In the midst of all that we know is going on in our world—war, poverty, racism, destruction of the environment—how do we rejoice?

First of all, the joy that Paul is talking about is an emotion and something far deeper than emotion. It is a way of looking at reality; it is a stance toward the world; it is a lens through which to see beneath the surface to deeper truth. In his exhortation, Paul challenges his friends to "rejoice in the Lord." Joy is not abstract; it is grounded in the simple but stunning truth that only God is God. When the Christian confesses that Jesus Christ is Lord, it is a way of saying who is *not*. None of the things we think of as sovereign over life really are. Evil, suffering, and death will not have the last word. The last word will come from the One who spoke the first word, the good and gracious God who made us and all things, the God whose name is love.

Second, Paul's exhortation to rejoice is a call for us to recognize who we are as creatures made in the image and likeness of God. The authors of the Westminster Shorter Catechism open with this question: "What is the chief end of [humanity]? [Humankind's] chief end is to glorify God and to enjoy him forever." What does this mean? How do we "enjoy" God? Another way to express this idea is to say that God is the supreme good and that in seeking and finding God, we realize our true destiny. We find ourselves, our true selves, as we draw closer to God. We are most fully human when we recognize ourselves as the image of the loving Creator.

Many theologians today use the language of "human flourishing" to describe what the authors of Westminster were getting at. In the biblical view of creation, God made everything abundantly and richly good. Humans were intended to live and to thrive in harmony with nature and with one another in a beautiful and verdant garden. The Christian Bible concludes with the vision of evelation: a city, a place where humans live together, that is in reality a fruitful, watered garden. When Paul exhorts us to "rejoice in the Lord," he urges us to remember who we really are and to live our lives in ways that celebrate the true beauty and goodness of creation.

The Church: Rejoice . . . Always?

Paul's words in 4:4–7 are some of the most beloved in all of Scripture. They appear in the lectionary in Advent and on Thanksgiving

Day. They are read frequently at both weddings and funerals. Many people commit these words to memory and find in them great comfort and encouragement, particularly in times of danger or distress. Paul's assurance that "the Lord is near" (or at hand) echoes the words of Psalm 23: "Yea, though I walk through the valley of the shadow of death, I will fear no evil: for thou art with me; thy rod and thy staff they comfort me" (v. 4 KJV).

These words are also a primer for prayer. Prayer begins as we place ourselves consciously in God's presence. God is always near, even if we are not aware of it. Prayer begins when we welcome God into our hearts. Paul urges us to set aside worry. Clearly, Paul knows that he has a great deal about which to worry—he is in prison, after all. Paul encourages us not to be anxious about things that God knows that we need. As Jesus taught: "Do not worry about your life, what you will eat, or about your body, what you will wear. For life is more than food, and the body more than clothing" (Luke 12:22–23). Neither Jesus nor Paul romanticizes suffering; they do not deny the injustice of poverty or violence. But when we place our trust in God, we can be free from debilitating anxiety and thus open to facing the real challenges that life presents.

Paul then urges us to present our whole selves and all the concerns of our hearts to God: "in everything by prayer and supplication with thanksgiving let your requests be made known to God" (Philippians 4:6). God already knows our deepest longings (and fears); in prayer, we bring them to our consciousness as well as God's. We place our prayers for healing and help, for justice and peace, for protection for ourselves and others, all in God's loving and powerful presence. But notice that Paul says that all our requests should be framed with thanksgiving. Gratitude for what God has already done in creation and in our lives is the beginning and the end of prayer. We are not to pray while fearful of God's response. We are to pray with confidence because of God's grace and steadfast love, which endure forever.

This kind of prayer receives a blessing, Paul says: "The peace of God, which surpasses all understanding, will guard your hearts and minds in Christ Jesus" (v. 7). There is an echo here of the great benediction in Numbers 6:24–26: "The LORD bless you and keep you; . . . the LORD lift up his countenance upon you, and give you peace." Fred Craddock suggests that the word "guard" means "stand sentry watch." In Paul's prison, it is not the Roman guards who keep watch, but God, whose presence is at hand. "Because God's peace is on duty, [we] do not have to be anxiously scanning the horizon for new threats," Craddock writes.[1] Cause for rejoicing indeed.

Spiritual Practice

If you have not done so already, memorize 4:4–7. Repeat it slowly as you begin your prayer time each day. Notice what word or words stand out for you. After you have reflected on that word or phrase, write your thoughts in a journal. Review the journal at the end of the week.

For Reflection and Action

1. What do you think it was about Paul's preaching that was so disruptive that it led to his arrest? Is there anything in the preaching of your congregation that might lead to arrest? Should there be?

2. Do you know someone who has a joy-filled outlook on life? What are the characteristics of that person? What does it mean to look at life through the lens of joy?

3. Paul suggests that all our prayers of petition and intercession be framed in gratitude. How does this fit with your prayer practice? What difference might it make to follow Paul's suggestion?

1. Fred B. Craddock, *Philippians*, Interpretation: A Bible Commentary for Teaching and Preaching (Louisville, KY: Westminster John Knox Press, 2012), 72.

*Whoever professes Christ as Lord can only do so
legitimately by patterning one's life on Christ: the
one who emptied himself and gave his life for the
whole world; who welcomed those on the margins of
his society, who came not to be served but to serve.*

Chapter 3

Beliefs That Matter

Scripture
Philippians 2:5–11   One of the most famous passages in this
letter is the hymn in chapter 2 that describes the "self-emptying"
Christ. This chapter reflects on the implication of that vision of
Christ for us as we seek to follow him.

Prayer
Help us, dear God, to open our hearts and minds so that the mind
of Christ will dwell in us, transform us, and draw us closer to one
another and to you. Amen.

Introduction
Philippians 2:5–11 is generally thought to be a hymn that was well-
known both to Paul and to the community in Philippi. We assume
that early Christian communities used biblical psalms in worship
and found in them ways to interpret and express their faith in
Christ. But Christians also began to compose their own hymns,
and this appears to be one of them. The nineteenth-century hymn
"At the Name of Jesus" (set to the majestic tune by Ralph Vaughan
Williams) is a paraphrase of this text, perhaps giving us a feel for
what the Philippians experienced when using this hymn.

   This passage has become a fixture in the Christian lectionary and is in the Revised Common Lectionary for every Palm (or

Passion) Sunday. It tells the story of Jesus in three movements: coequal with God; self-emptying to become incarnate, suffer, and die; exalted to reign over all. Although Paul's reason for quoting the hymn was more ethical than theological (as we shall see in the next chapter), this hymn has figured prominently in debates about the person and nature of Christ.

Other theological claims made by this hymn would have been both provocative and controversial at the time. First, the hymn makes use of the title "lord," which was used for the Roman emperor. (Another title given to the emperor was "savior.") To declare that someone else was "savior and lord" would have been tantamount to blasphemy and sedition. Second, the hymn suggests that believers owe loyalty or allegiance solely to Christ. The idea that there is only one God and that all others held up as gods are idols was a key concept in Jewish faith. But in the Greco-Roman world, multiple deities were worshiped, and most cities, including Philippi, had a wide range of religious practice. In that light, Christian exclusivism seemed strange, unpatriotic, and perhaps even dangerous or subversive.

A Basic Theme: Theology in Poetry

Who is Jesus Christ? What does it mean to call Jesus the "Son of God" and to address prayers to him? If there is only one God, then how are the Creator and Jesus both God? These questions are as old as Christian faith and as fresh as the reflections of each believer. As we will see in the next chapter, however, Paul is not first of all trying to answer these deep theological questions. He is speaking to the congregation about how they are getting along with each other (or not!) and reminding them of a favorite hymn to encourage them to improve their behavior.

Nevertheless, the theological claims of the hymn itself have figured prominently in theological debates about the person and nature of Christ. The first idea we meet is *preexistence*. The hymn says that Christ shared equality (and thus life) with God prior to the incarnation. We find the same idea in John 1:1 ("In the beginning was the Word, and the Word was with God, and the Word was God"). Such statements about Christ seem to have their roots in the figure of Wisdom (or Lady Wisdom) in Proverbs (see 8:22–31) and other Old Testament writings. This idea is important because it implies that when God became incarnate in Jesus of Nazareth, this was not an afterthought or plan B when plan A didn't work out. The Son, who became human in Jesus, has always been God. God has always been what we see in Jesus.

The second idea is the pattern of *humiliation and exaltation*. The hymn itself is in two stanzas. The first concerns the self-emptying of Christ in the incarnation. The second concerns the exaltation of Christ following the resurrection. The scandal of the cross was one of the major objections to believing in Christ. Why would you worship as a god someone who was humiliated by crucifixion? Romans reserved crucifixion as a form of capital punishment for those it deemed to be the most politically dangerous offenders. The point was not just to torture the victim. Crucifixion was a public spectacle, and the point was death by humiliation. This hymn is fully consistent with Paul's theology that the weakness of the cross actually displays the power of God. What looks like a scandal and a stumbling block is, in fact, the means of our salvation.

The third idea is that the one who was crucified is now raised to *rule the entire universe*. The death and resurrection of Jesus has changed everything. Jesus is the firstfruits of the new age that God has promised. The reign of God, long anticipated by the prophets of ancient Israel, has begun to break into human history. Those who come to faith in Christ participate now in the new life that eventually will spread to the whole creation. The hymn concludes with a vision of the consummation of history in which all creation acknowledges that the One who reigns is the One who emptied himself for the sake of all.

The Life of Faith: Beliefs That Matter

If it is true that Jesus is "the human face of God," then what does this picture of Christ show us about God's character? What does it mean to believe in a self-emptying God? Among the many important implications of this startling picture, we will reflect on two. First, this amazing hymn makes clear that sacrificial love is at the heart of the divine character. Second, God's self-emptying in Christ radically redefines our ideas of power and authority.

For many centuries, Christian thought was heavily influenced by Greek philosophy. According to that way of thinking, God is (by definition) what humans are *not*: we are finite creatures bound by time; God is infinite and eternal. We grow and change; God is unchanging. For many centuries, language about God was highly abstract. The definition of God in the Westminster Larger Catechism is a good example: "God is a Spirit, in and of himself infinite in being, glory, blessedness, and perfection; all-sufficient, eternal, unchangeable, incomprehensible, everywhere present, almighty. . . ." All of this was a way of thinking about God's perfection (in contrast to our imperfection) and God's otherness in contrast to God's creation.

The hymn in Philippians presents a very different picture. Although Christ (present with God from the beginning) is equal to God, Christ "empties himself" of all that fullness of divine reality and comes into the world of humanity. This incredible act of self-giving (which climaxes in death on the cross) is anticipated in Jesus' own words: "If any want to become my followers, let them deny themselves and take up their cross and follow me. For those who want to save their life will lose it, and those who lose their life for my sake, and for the sake of the gospel, will save it" (Mark 8:34–35). In the Gospel of John, this act of self-giving becomes the model for Christ's definition of love: "This is my commandment, that you love one another as I have loved you. No one has greater love than this, to lay down one's life for one's friends" (John 15:12–13). In this way, Christ becomes the window onto the true heart of God: self-sacrificial love, freely given for the life of the world.

The self-emptying Christ is a picture of holy love, but it is also a redefinition of divine power. When we think of power, we generally think of "power over"—the ability to exert influence or control so that an individual or business or nation gets what it wants. Power is what wins; power is strength; power dominates. Many of the psalms present this image of divine power: God is the strong ruler, the one who protects and defends God's people, Israel.

The picture of the Philippians' hymn turns this image upside down and inside out. Here, God is defined by the act of giving away, of surrendering power and authority and influence in favor of solidarity with frail humanity. This image also has Old Testament roots, specifically in the Suffering Servant as described by Isaiah: "He was despised and rejected by others; a man of suffering and acquainted with infirmity; as one from whom others hide their faces he was despised, and we held him of no account" (Isaiah 53:3). And yet this is the one who carries the people's sins and who becomes the path to redemption. Power is redefined by willingness to suffer for others.

The Church: Whom Do We Worship?

The Philippians' hymn was controversial in the first century, and it remains challenging to us today in at least two ways. First, this text urges us to consider who it is that commands our highest allegiance; to whom or what do we owe the greatest loyalty? Theologian Paul Tillich wrote that faith is not best understood as a system of theological ideas or beliefs. Faith is our "ultimate concern"—where we place our deepest trust in life. Only when we place our ultimate concern in something that is truly ultimate (that is, in God) will we fulfill our human identity. The problem, Tillich went on to say, is that all too often we give our ultimate loyalty to things that are not ultimate. Tillich was a refugee from Nazi Germany. He had fought in World War I, and he saw Hitler and Nazi ideology as an idol—something that was not God but that claimed God's place in human hearts and minds.

John Calvin famously said that the human heart is a "factory of idols." Calvin and many of his contemporaries were concerned that statues of saints and even stained-glass windows might be seen as holy in and of themselves rather than as things that point us to the Holy One. But his concern was deeper than that. Calvin was trying to remind us that only God is God and that when we put anything else in God's place, no matter how good that thing may be, we are guilty of idolatry and we are on a path that leads to death. Our "gods" may be nationalism or our net worth or personal success or even family. But each of those (even at their very best) is only a proximate good, not the ultimate good. Idols disappoint. Only God is God, the only source of life.

The other challenge of this hymn is the claim of Christian exclusivism. The last stanza proclaims that God exalted Christ "so that at the name of Jesus every knee should bend, . . . and every tongue should confess that Jesus Christ is Lord, to the glory of God the Father." Clearly, what makes us Christian is to affirm that Jesus Christ is Savior and Lord, the source of life and the one who commands our ultimate loyalty. But how do we hold this confession in tension with a desire to live respectfully and at peace with our neighbors from different religious traditions?

We live in a very different context from the world in which Paul lived. We know all too well the threats to peace that can arise from religious exclusivism. We also have good biblical reasons for affirming that God has made all humanity in God's own image and that God loves all that God has made. Whoever professes Christ as Lord can only do so legitimately by patterning one's life on Christ: the one who did not hold on to power but emptied himself and gave his life for the whole world; who welcomed those on the margins of his society, including those from outside the faith tradition of Israel; who came not to be served but to serve.

Spiritual Practice
Do a "loyalty inventory" by making a list of the things to which you are committed. This may include marriage, family, and children; your profession and its standards of conduct; your personal life goals; civic, social, or political organizations or causes. How are these loyalties related to your loyalty to God?

For Reflection and Action
1. What does it mean to you to understand the nature of God through the lens of the life, death, and resurrection of Jesus? How does that help you read or interpret other parts of the Bible?

2. We often address God as "almighty" or as "sovereign." How do you hold those ideas in relationship to the "self-emptying" picture in the Philippians' hymn?

3. What are some appropriate ways of affirming that Jesus is Lord in a world of religious diversity?

When we share the mind of Christ, we can come to embrace the differences among us, knowing that we all belong to God.

Chapter 4

Being of One Mind

Scripture
Philippians 2:1–5, 12–17   Paul urges the Philippians to be united or "of the same mind" with one another. This chapter explores various challenges we face as we try to live in community while honoring diversity.

Prayer
Dear God, you have made us to be members of one body in Jesus Christ. Open our hearts and minds to discover this new reality and to deepen the ties that bind us to one another and to Christ. Amen.

Introduction
I am always amazed when people are surprised by church conflict. The church is not a refuge for the pure so that they can remain uncontaminated. The church is the haven of sinners who are willing to acknowledge their brokenness and be open to transformation. The goal of the Christian life is not perfection; it is the process of being reconciled again and again and again.

Churches deal with conflict in a variety of ways, depending on how they understand what it means to be church. Some parts of the church value complete agreement on precise theological doctrine or moral principles and remove those who do not comply.

Other parts of the church value consensus nearly above all else and have devised practices designed to achieve it. Other churches are democratic systems where decisions, even on matters of theology and ethics, are made by majority rule.

We may think of church conflict as a modern problem, but Scripture tells us otherwise. Conflict arose among Jesus' own disciples (James and John wanted places of honor next to Jesus in glory, sparking resentment among the others). Conflict abounded in the early Christian movement, as almost all of Paul's letters reflect. Sometimes the issues are clear: both Galatians and Romans reflect deep disagreements over how the provisions of Torah (especially regarding circumcision and dietary laws) applied to non-Jewish Christians. In Corinth, there were disputes about moral issues, worship practices, and leadership. Other times, the specifics are less obvious, but Paul's attempt is always to bring fractured communities back together.

Paul's Letter to the Philippians gives the least evidence of conflict of all of Paul's correspondence. In the first chapter, we noticed the reference to the conflict between two leaders, Euodia and Syntyche (4:2). In 1:15–17 and 3:2, Paul seems to be referring to rival Christian teachers whose influence may be causing division in the church. But whatever the issues, Paul calls for his friends in Philippi to be reconciled and introduces the intriguing metaphor of being "of one mind."

A Basic Theme: The Mind of Christ

In the last chapter, we examined the so-called Christ hymn in 2:5–11 and explored the ways in which that text shows us Paul's vision of the self-giving love of God in Christ. Now we turn to the reason why Paul reminds his readers of their familiar and possibly favorite song. He is not first of all concerned about theology; his primary concern is how this community is getting along (or not!).

Here is another translation of 2:1–4, by Bonnie Thurston: "Therefore if [there is] any comfort in Christ, if any consolation of love, if any fellowship of spirit, if any compassion and tenderness, fulfill my joy, having the same opinions, the same love, one-souled, thinking the one [thing], [doing] nothing from selfish ambition, nothing from empty glory, but in humility counting others superior to yourselves, each one not considering the things of themselves, but [also] the things of others."[1]

The key word here is *phronete*, which the NRSV translates "be of the same mind." This term is used twenty-three times by Paul and at least ten times in Philippians. Thurston translates this "thinking the one" or the same thing. Those who have the same mind share an outlook or disposition toward life. It goes deeper than opinion and suggests that those of the same mind share a pattern of behavior or way of engaging the world.

Paul also describes this way of life in the negative: "Do nothing from selfish ambition or conceit." This may be the root of the problem in Philippi: people are vying with one another for leadership or competing for attention. Then Paul makes the point in the positive: "Regard others as better than yourselves" and "look . . . to the interests of others." Another way of saying this, of course, is to "love your neighbor as yourself." This way of engaging one another and the world is summed up for Paul in the pattern of Christ's life, death, and resurrection. The self-emptying, self-giving love described in the hymn is the mind-set that Paul wants his friends to share.

Many rightly point out that this language has been misused almost as much as it has been used rightly. When this notion of considering others better than oneself is used as a way to assign permanent subordinate status to some and superior status to others (women in relation to men; persons of color in relation to whites; poor in relation to rich), this is completely counter to Paul's meaning. The "self-emptying" pattern is that of Christ who *knows* that his true identity is "equality with God." Our true identity is as those created in God's own image and likeness. It is on this basis of equal standing that we are then invited into a mind of radical mutuality and communion.

The Life of Faith: What Is the Nature of the Unity We Seek?

In this letter, there seem to be two threats to the community: internal disagreement and external persecution. Evidence of the first is found in 3:2: "Beware of the dogs, beware of the evil workers, beware of those who mutilate the flesh!" Evidently there were

---

1 Bonnie B. Thurston and Judith M. Ryan, *Philippians & Philemon*, Sacra Pagina 10 (Collegeville, MN: Liturgical Press, 2005), 72.

people teaching things other than Paul's version of the gospel. Paul is probably referring to the issue that figures prominently in Galatians, namely, whether Gentile men need to be circumcised (that is, enter the covenant of Israel) in order to become Christian. Whatever the issues, we know that at least two key leaders are at odds with each other (see 4:2, "I urge Euodia and I urge Syntyche to be *of the same mind* in the Lord").

There is also the problem of persecution or pressure from outside. Paul himself is in prison. Not only is this evidence of official opposition, but it also raises the specter that what happened to Paul could happen also to them. Paul takes great pains to reassure the Philippians by saying that his imprisonment "has actually helped to spread the gospel" (1:12). But reassurances would not be necessary if people were not anxious. Paul's concern is that internal disagreements or the creation of factions could lead to the larger community having a lower opinion of Christians, which could, in turn, lead to persecution.

What is the nature of the unity that Paul urges, and why is unity so important? First of all, he does not seem to be emphasizing agreement about theological ideas or doctrines. The allusion to "false teachers" is almost a passing comment. Neither does he seem to be emphasizing social conformity. Paul's desire for this community is not just that it have "the *same* mind" but that it have "the mind of *Christ*." In all of his writing, Paul is clear that being a Christian means being "in Christ" in relationship to others who share the faith.

To put it another way, when someone receives baptism, that person enters into a new community (the body of Christ), and this community fundamentally reorders that person's relationships with others. In fact, Christian community was nothing short of revolutionary. Being "in Christ" meant being in community with people from different ethnicities (Jews, Greeks, Romans, etc.) and different social and economic status (slaves and owners). Women as well as men (at least in the early days) were in leadership. The differences created by human society and custom were transcended by the conviction that all were "the same" in Christ, beloved children of God redeemed by the grace of Christ.

The unity that Paul envisions is grounded in and shaped by Christ and his way of being in the world. It is Christ who is to be the pattern for how people relate to one another in this new community. Because he did not put his own interests first, but rather lived and died for the sake of a broken humanity, those who live in him are to make service to others their first priority.

The Church: Unity, Diversity, and Community

How much diversity (of opinion or practice) can an organization (or church or nation) tolerate and remain united? For its first thousand years, Christianity had quite a good deal of regional variation but was essentially one movement. Now it is splintered into literally thousands of pieces. No one even tried to put some of those pieces back together until the twentieth century. What divides the universal church? And what could unite it?

The motto of the United States is *E pluribus unum*, "Out of many, one." And we were one until we weren't. Are we still "one nation, indivisible"? Our recent history finds us deeply divided not only by political ideology but also by race, economic class, gender identity, and more. Finding common ground not only is difficult but also is not even particularly valued.

Some suggest that the root of our modern divisions can be traced to an overemphasis on individualism that has flourished in recent decades. According to this line of thinking, when we make individual achievement or personal success our primary goal, we are in danger of forgetting that we, humans, are fundamentally relational beings. Both psychologists and theologians affirm that "it is not good that the human be alone" (cf. Genesis 2:18). Human beings are literally dependent on others for years until they are able to survive on their own, and relationships with others are absolutely critical to personal development. The idea of being a "self-made" person is simply contrary to fact, and continuing to value that idea is detrimental to the health of human communities.

Christianity is a religion of belonging. Baptism makes a collection of individuals into the living body of Christ on earth. No part of the body can say to another part, "I have no need of you" (1 Corinthians 12:21). Nor do any parts of the body continue to exist unless they are attached to the others, and especially to the brain or "the head," as Paul calls Christ. The beauty of this image is that it encompasses both unity and diversity. The body is one, but it is made up of a huge diversity of parts, and it does not function well unless all those parts or members are thriving in their own right.

In this "broken and fearful world,"[2] this sense of community may be the greatest gift Christians have to offer the neighborhoods, cities, and nation in which we live. Congregations are places to practice not only mutual care and support but also mutual forbearance. We practice making decisions for the common good. We support programs that we don't necessarily participate in, because we know that others benefit from them. We know that belonging is deeper than agreeing. We practice intergenerational understanding.

Living with difference has never been easy. The key is embracing what we all share in common: namely, that we are all beloved children of God, bearers of the divine image, and redeemed by the love of Jesus Christ. When we share the mind of Christ, we can come to embrace the differences among us, knowing that we all belong to God.

Spiritual Practice
Seek out someone with whom you disagree and try to discover areas of common ground. Are there values you share or ways that you would like to see your community improve (even if you have different ways to approach the problems)? Try to listen deeply to the other person's concerns and fears.

For Reflection and Action
1. What has been your experience of conflict in the church? How was it handled well? How could it have been handled more effectively?

2. The Presbyterian Church (U.S.A.) *Book of Order* says that when elders and ministers of the Word and Sacrament come together in the councils of the church (session, presbytery, and General Assembly), they are to seek together to discern "the mind of Christ." How have you experienced that or observed it?

2. "A Brief Statement of Faith," in *The Constitution of the Presbyterian Church (U.S.A.),* Part 1, *Book of Confessions* (Louisville, KY: Office of the General Assembly, Presbyterian Church (U.S.A.), 2016), 11.4.

3. Are there ways in which the church makes decisions or welcomes diversity that could be helpful to life in society? Are there things about welcoming diversity that the church might learn from other organizations?

Our identity as Christians is not like a card we keep in our wallet and produce only on demand. It is not only about believing (in the sense of having the right ideas) but also about behaving—living in ways that give evidence of relationship with Christ.

Chapter 5

Christian Identity

Scripture
Philippians 1:20–21; 3:7–4:1   For Paul, being a Christian is more than following the teachings of Jesus. It involves a profound, spiritual union with Christ. This chapter invites us to explore our own journeys of faith and the practices that might deepen our relationship with Christ.

Prayer
O Christ, help us to see you more clearly, love you more dearly, and follow you more nearly, day by day. Amen.

Introduction
What does it mean to be a Christian? This is undoubtedly the most fundamental question that we ask. When a child is baptized as an infant, a congregation promises to help the family raise her so that she will come to know and follow Christ. When a young person goes through a confirmation class, he comes to a new and deeper level of understanding and commitment. Hopefully, as adults, we never cease to ask this question of ourselves: what *does* it mean to be a Christian?

The writings of Paul represent the first recorded attempts to answer this question, and his experience has exerted powerful influence on Christians for centuries. For Paul, the answer is not first of all

27

to follow the teachings of Jesus. He assumes, I think, that his audience knows what Jesus taught, and so he spends no time rehearsing that material. Rather, Paul presents a picture of a transformed identity. To be a Christian is to become a new person "in Christ." The one who has faith in Christ is transformed, Paul says, into the image and likeness of Christ. But "faith," for Paul, is far more than *beliefs about* Christ. It is really better understood as *trust in* or *loyalty to* him. Indeed, our faith *in* Christ is made possible by the faith *of* Christ: because of Christ's faithfulness (or obedience) to God, we are able to be faithful (loyal and trusting) to him.

This idea of Christian identity is a central topic of this brief letter to the church in Philippi. Paul's context in writing is key to understanding his message. Paul is in prison, and his fate is far from certain. We know that he will be released and able to continue his work for many years. But for now, he is enduring the anxiety of being confined and the threat of death. But what he fears more than death is that he will be "put to shame," that he will lack the courage needed to hold fast under duress. It appears that some have suggested that Paul's imprisonment is a sign of the deficiency of his message, so his tone here is defensive. But his goal is to express his transformation in solidarity with Christ.

A Basic Theme: "Living Is Christ" (1:21)
Paul does not ever tell his readers how he came to faith in Christ. He never shares his own version of the Damascus Road experience that is told in Acts 9. What he does describe is coming to embrace a new identity given to him by his identification with Christ and, in particular, by sharing in Christ's suffering (which was in Paul's mind the key to Christ's obedience to God). As Paul sees it, the goal of life is to be found "righteous" or to live in right relationship with God. In his previous life, Paul understood that one attained righteousness by observing the law of Moses. Paul never repudiates the content of the law of Moses. What he comes to see is that, for him, a life based on rigorous observance of either moral or doctrinal rules led to a logic of achievement: *I* did this; *I* kept the law; *I* was faithful. As he says, he was "as to righteousness under the law, blameless" (Philippians 3:6).

Instead of seeing right relationship with God as something to be attained, Paul came to see that it was a gift bestowed by God because of Christ's faithful obedience. For this, Paul is willing to give up all claims of his own. He is willing to set aside all his intellectual and moral achievements. "I regard them as rubbish, in order that I may gain Christ and be found in him, not having a righteousness of my own that comes from the law, but one that comes *through the faith of Christ*" (vv. 8–9).

Most English translations provide this version in the footnotes, and it is a point of translation that makes a very big difference. The Greek preposition can be translated either "in" or "of." So, which is it? Are we made righteous (or set right with God) because of *our* faith *in* Christ (that is, by believing)? Or are we made righteous (set right with God) because of the faith (the faithful obedience) *of* Christ? In light of all that Paul says, it seems that the latter reading is closer to what he intends. Being set back into right relationship with God is not something we do or can achieve. It is God's gift to us made known in and through the faithfulness that Jesus shows us through his life and especially through his death.

What does it mean to be a Christian? It means to share in the life of Christ by living as he lived, in complete obedience to God. For Jesus, this meant suffering persecution and rejection and eventually execution. Paul sees his own suffering, and now his imprisonment and possibly impending death, as a participation in Christ's own suffering. And, in a way that may seem difficult for us to comprehend, Paul sees this as a privilege. His imprisonment is not a "shame." It is solidarity with the One whose faithfulness has brought him freedom, new life, and (as he says more than once in this letter) deep joy.

The Life of Faith: "Pressing On toward the Goal"

Paul uses another metaphor for right relationship with God, and that is to "attain the resurrection" (v. 11). What he means by this is living the new life liberated from the power of sin and the threat of death. Obviously, we will not share in the fullness of right relationship or resurrected life until the day when God makes all things new, but we can participate in the resurrection now, and that takes work. Here, Paul compares it to runners competing in a race: "Forgetting what lies behind and straining forward to what lies ahead, I press on toward the goal for the prize of the heavenly call of God in Christ Jesus" (3:13–14). Being reconciled to God is indeed a gift we receive through God's grace, but living into our new identity takes hard work. We press on, Paul says, like the runner who desperately wants to cross the finish line and claim the prize, as he doubtless saw at countless public games in the cities he visited.

How can our new identity in Christ be a gift *and* something we must strive for? Isn't this a fundamental contradiction? The contradiction resolves as we realize that God's gift of new life is what makes it possible for us to strive to grow up into the identity we have been given. Having been set free from thinking of right relationship with God as something we earn, we are now able to learn how to practice the faith at new and deeper levels as we grow and grow up. We are free to seek God because we know that we have already been found.

This is the point of "spiritual disciplines." Our identity as Christians is not like a card we keep in our wallet and produce only upon demand. Our new life in Christ is always a "work in progress." It is not only about believing (in the sense of having the right ideas) but also about behaving—living in ways that give evidence of relationship with Christ. Those who have gone before us in the faith have discerned that there are a variety of practices that, engaged in over time, deepen our trust in Christ and make us more like him. These include regularly reading and studying the Scriptures, praying, sharing our possessions, and extending hospitality.

For Paul, the prize at the end of the race is new life in Christ. We do not earn that prize by running the fastest. Discipleship is not a competition. But by running the race that Jesus himself ran (pouring out his life as a testimony to divine love), our lives are transformed more and more into Christ. Thankfully, we do not do this alone. The church is rightly understood as the school of faith (or perhaps the gym, in keeping with Paul's metaphor of the race). Here, we train alongside one another, encouraging each other, as our daily living comes to a deeper reflection of God's love in Christ.

Spiritual Practice
Several spiritual disciplines—Bible study, prayer, charity, and hospitality—are listed above. Select one and find time each day to engage in that practice. Reflect at the end of the week on what you experienced.

For Reflection and Action

1. How do you tell the story of your own faith journey? When did faith begin for you? What are some of the ups and downs that you have experienced? Where are you now?

2. What aspects of the life and ministry of Jesus are most important to you as you reflect on shaping your life after his?

3. What do you make of the distinction between the faith *of* Christ (or Christ's faithfulness) and faith *in* Christ? How is faith both something that we are given and something for which we strive?

Generosity goes beyond financial and material support.
True generosity is also a matter of the spirit and shapes how
we encounter others. The generous heart sees the best in the
other and seeks their well-being as well as one's own. These
are practices that lead to abundant life.

Chapter 6

Mutual Hospitality

Scripture
Acts 16:9–15, 40; Philippians 2:25–30; 4:15–20   Paul's ministry in Philippi began when he accepted the hospitality extended to him by his first follower, Lydia. This chapter invites us to reflect on the practices of generosity and hospitality as expressions of Christian faith.

Prayer
Dear God, as you opened Lydia's heart to receive the good news, open our eyes to see you in all we meet. Amen.

Introduction
Decades before the Christian movement adapted itself to traditional Greco-Roman patriarchal norms, there were glimmers of a different way of life, a new type of community. Even though the full story is lost, names are remembered. Paul does not mention Lydia by name in his Letter to the Philippians, but her story recounted in Acts is an important backdrop for the letter as a whole. It's amazing how much we know about Lydia from the brief description. She lives in Philippi, but she is originally from Thyatira, in what is now Turkey. She owns her own home and is head of a household, unusual for a woman but not unheard of. She is a merchant who specializes in purple cloth, the very expensively dyed fabric that

only the elites in Roman society were permitted to wear. She is also a "God-fearer." This is a specific term for a non-Jewish person who is drawn to the faith community of Israel but has not converted to Judaism. She is a seeker. God opens her heart to receive the good news, and thus Lydia becomes the first person in Europe to be baptized.

There are lots of conversion stories in Acts (e.g., Cornelius the Roman army officer and the Ethiopian court official), but they all end with baptism. In the story of Lydia, we see what her life looks like after baptism. Having embraced the good news of God's grace in Jesus, Lydia opened her home to Paul: she *urged* Paul and his companions to come to her home, and she *prevailed*. Thus, Lydia's home became the base of operations for Paul, and it became the first "house church" of Philippi. Lydia's hospitality gave birth to the church in Europe, and in all likelihood, Lydia became its first pastor/leader, since that was the customary role of the one in whose home the community met.

The beginning of the Christian community in Philippi sets the stage for the mutuality of hospitality that we see in Paul's letter written some years later. In this session, we explore the ways in which hospitality is at the heart of both the gospel and discipleship.

A Basic Theme: Hospitality, a Two-Way Street
At first glance, it might seem that the practice of hospitality creates an unequal relationship: one is the host, the other the guest. One gives, the other receives. But in fact, hospitality is more complex than that. When it is done properly, hospitality becomes a real relationship in which both parties are mutually engaged, mutually benefit, and are mutually transformed. Lydia's hospitality to Paul laid the foundation for a relationship of giving and receiving that shapes the Philippian church.

On one level, Paul is the "benefactor." He is the one who creates this community through his preaching and teaching. This was Paul's ministry: to found communities, to raise up leadership from within the group, and then to move on. We know that his goal was to eventually visit the Christian community in Rome on his way to planting more churches in Spain. The core of his message was that, through Christ, the door was now open to all people to become children of God and heirs of the promise of mercy and grace. Paul was clearly the "giver," the host welcoming women and men into the family of God.

At least in Philippi, however, the welcome Paul extended was returned as this community responded with deep generosity. Once the church in Philippi was well-enough established, Paul moved on to Thessalonica (the community to which he would eventually write his first letters). It is evident from this letter that Paul's ministry there was made possible in large part by the Philippians: "When I left Macedonia, no church shared with me in the matter of giving and receiving, except you alone. For even when I was in Thessalonica, you sent me help for my needs more than once" (4:15–16). Clearly, the Philippians had embraced the practice of sharing what they have and contributing to the welfare of others.

Apparently this relationship continued for many years. At the writing of this letter, Paul is in prison and is being cared for by a man named Epaphroditus. Philippians 2 tells us that Epaphroditus is a member of the Philippian church who has been sent by them to support Paul during his incarceration. Somehow during this time Epaphroditus became gravely ill, causing great concern for his friends back in Philippi. Now that he has recovered, Paul is sending him back home, deeply grateful for the ways in which he has been ministered to by this friend and, by extension, by the whole Philippian community.

The good news of the gospel is that God in Jesus Christ welcomes all. Among the Philippians, that message became the hallmark of their collective discipleship. Because of the grace extended to them, they became benefactors of others. What they did for Paul was likely typical of what they believed they were called to do for others in need. In receiving, they discovered the call to give. In all of this, we see that the gospel is not only a way of thinking about or understanding God but also a way of life that mirrors the divine generosity.

The Life of Faith: The "Disciplined" Life

In recent years, the concept of "spiritual disciplines" or "spiritual practices" has found a ready audience among Protestants. The idea that living a Christian life involves various practices (such as praying, fasting, giving alms, and going on pilgrimage) has its roots in Judaism and has been a mainstay of Catholic Christianity for centuries. Many Protestants, however, were raised to be wary of these activities as "works righteousness," or doing certain things so as to earn God's favor or merit God's grace.

Fortunately, a number of pastors and teachers began to help us see spiritual disciplines as they were always intended: not as a means to earn God's grace but rather as our appropriate response to grace in ways that draw us more deeply into God's presence. Often the analogy is made to health and fitness. A healthy lifestyle is far more than learning about health or understanding the concepts of physical wellness. Being healthy involves various practices of diet, exercise, rest, and mental stimulation. We become healthier by engaging in healthy practices. So also with the spiritual life. We deepen our relationship with God by practicing things that draw us closer to God.

Some spiritual disciplines are obvious. If we want to deepen our relationship with God, we need to spend time with God in prayer and in reflection on God's word in Scripture. But there are other disciplines that are equally important. The example of the Philippian community suggests two: hospitality and generosity.

One of the most influential guides to living the Christian life is the *Rule of St. Benedict*. Written more than fifteen hundred years ago, this brief manual was created to shape monastic life for men and women who sought to dedicate their lives to God, but its teaching reached far beyond the monastery. One of the most basic rules that Benedict set forth was that all who came to the monastery were to be welcomed as Christ. That is, the community was to receive every person who showed up on their doorstep as if Jesus were standing before them. The same hospitality was to be shown to all, rich and poor alike. All were to be received as Christ himself.

The second discipline, closely related, is generosity. When we recognize that all that we are and all that we have is a free gift from God, we understand that we are the recipients of God's incredible generosity. We do not deserve God's love; we cannot earn God's grace; and yet it has been poured into our hearts in baptism and nurtured each time we come to the Lord's Table. Such divine generosity compels us to respond in kind.

Generosity comes in many forms. If we have resources, we are to share what we have with those in need. This is what the

Philippians did time and again for Paul, and for this he is deeply grateful. Generosity goes beyond financial and material support. True generosity is also a matter of the spirit and shapes how we encounter others. The generous heart sees the best in the other and seeks their well-being as well as one's own. These are practices that lead to abundant life.

The Church: Shaping a Hospitable World

All congregations want to be (and most believe they are!) welcoming to all. But as most churches know, being welcoming is not easy. Many church members know where they want to sit for worship. Visitors arrive and sit in those seats. Even if members are really glad the visitors are there, they experience (and sometimes show) a sense of disruption. When I was at McCormick Theological Seminary, I welcomed the new class each fall and said, "We are a new community now that you are here." We say it now in the congregation I serve. And it's true: when new people are welcomed into a congregation or school or business or club, the organization has been changed. The question is whether and how it welcomes these new people and the gifts (and changes) they bring.

The most revolutionary result of proclaiming the gospel was the creation of a new community where all were welcome: Jew *and* Gentile, slave *and* free, male *and* female. This vision of reaching across boundaries and barriers had its roots in the ministry of Jesus, who accepted the hospitality of all who invited him, whether they were religious leaders or "tax collectors and sinners"; who embraced those with leprosy; who welcomed women as friends and disciples. But Jesus did not invent the idea of broadening the vision of God's welcome. The roots of that moral vision are in the law of Moses. Over and over again, Israel is commanded to welcome the stranger and to provide for resident aliens. The reason given is that God reached out to care for Israel when they were strangers and slaves in Egypt. Extending hospitality to the outsider is at the heart of biblical faith.

Whom do we welcome and how? It is not only congregations that struggle with what it means to be hospitable. We struggle with this in neighborhoods and cities when we debate where affordable or low-income housing will be constructed or where to locate a halfway house for those being released from prison. We may want to be welcoming, but we worry about property values. As a nation, we are in the midst of a major debate about migration and immigration. Who should be able to come to the United States? What policies should govern how people attain citizenship? These are large and complex issues that need study and debate. But Christians should come to these conversations informed by the principles of generosity and hospitality we have explored in this chapter. If God has welcomed us freely in Christ into the household of God, how are we to extend that same welcome to others in Christ's name? And how will we be shaped and formed as we receive the gifts that others bring? These are profoundly spiritual questions.

Spiritual Practice
Before you go grocery shopping or run some other errand, take a few moments to center yourself and commit to looking at everyone you meet as Christ. When you get home, reflect on what difference that might have made in your interactions with others.

For Reflection and Action
1. How has your congregation or faith community changed as new members or participants have come to join? What gifts have they brought that have shaped the group in new ways?

2. What does it mean to live a generous life? What forms might generosity take for you individually and as a congregation?

3. What does Christian hospitality look like in the context of a global refugee crisis? What does it look like in a multi-faith world?

Group Gatherings

Eva Stimson

In This Together

Main Idea

Following Jesus means being in community. Paul's Letter to the Philippians shows his commitment to cultivating *koinonia*, or partnership, with followers of Jesus, including Lydia and other female leaders, who could strengthen the Christian community.

Preparing to Lead

- Read and reflect on chapter 1, "In This Together."
- Review this plan for the group gathering, and select questions and activities that you will use.
- What other questions, issues, or themes occur to you from your reflection?

Gathering

- Provide name tags and pens as people arrive.
- Provide simple refreshments; invite volunteers to bring refreshments for the next five gatherings.
- Agree on simple ground rules and organization (for example, time to begin and end; location for gatherings; welcoming of all points of view; confidentiality; and so on). Encourage participants to bring their study books and Bibles.
- Have available newsprint and markers.
- Review the gathering format: Gathering, Opening Worship, Conversation, and Conclusion.

Opening Worship

Prayer (unison)

Dear God, in Jesus Christ, you make us one with each other and with you. Help us to seek and find you in our communities of faith so that we may live as witnesses to your love for all. Amen.

Prayerful, Reflective Reading

- Read Philippians 1:3–7 aloud.
- Invite all to reflect for a few minutes in silence.
- After reflection time, invite all to listen for a word or phrase as the passage is read again and to reflect on that word or phrase in silence.
- Read the passage a third time, asking all to offer a silent prayer following the reading.
- Invite volunteers to share the word or phrase that spoke most deeply to them.

Prayer

Loving God, hear our prayers today as we seek to follow you more faithfully:

(*spoken prayers may be offered*)

Hear us now as we pray together, saying, Our Father . . .

Conversation

- Introduce chapter 1, "In This Together." Share observations, reflections, and insights.
- Invite participants to share something they know about their ancestry. Call attention to this statement: "Paul's letter to the community in Philippi is one window into our beginnings as Christians." For background on the letter, have someone read aloud Acts 16:11–15, 40. Review the Introduction (pp. 1–2). Ask:

    What do we know about Philippi in the time of Paul? About Lydia and her relationship with Paul?

- Review "A Basic Theme: *Koinonia*" (pp. 2–3). On a sheet of newsprint, write "koinonia." Invite participants to call out words or phrases that come to mind when they hear this Greek word. Write these on the newsprint. Note that koinonia implies working in partnership. Ask:

    Who were Paul's partners? (List them on the newsprint.) Which ones were women? (Put an asterisk beside each woman's name.)

    How does Philippians show partnership in action?

- Review "The Life of Faith: Partners in Ministry" (pp. 3–5). Share these key points:
  a. From the beginning, following Jesus meant being in community (Jesus called disciples; the early church prayed and broke bread together and cared for one another).
  b. Paul understood that ministry is never a solo venture. He engaged co-workers in the task of nurturing Christian community.

  It is striking that many of the leaders mentioned in Philippians are women. Ask:

  Does this surprise you? Why or why not? What does this letter suggest about Paul's views on women in leadership?

- Review "The Church: Embracing Common Life" (pp. 5–6). Ask:

  Why do you think so many people see faith as an individual journey or quest and feel no need to join a religious community?

Have participants divide into several small groups and discuss the questions in "For Reflection and Action" (p. 6). Ask someone from each group to record and report highlights of the discussion. Note common themes. Ask:

How can we nurture a stronger community in our congregation? In the larger church?

Conclusion

Read aloud Philippians 1:3–5. Invite participants to lift up prayers for people in your congregation, or use prayer suggestions from the *Book of Common Worship*, as suggested in "Spiritual Practice" (p. 6).

Passing the Peace

The peace of Christ be with you.
    And also with you.
Amen.

Great Joy

Main Idea

When Paul exhorts us to "rejoice in the Lord," he urges us to remember who we really are—creatures made in the image of God—and to live our lives in ways that celebrate the true beauty and goodness of creation, even in the midst of trials and suffering.

Preparing to Lead

- Read and reflect on chapter 2, "Great Joy."
- Review this plan for the group gathering, and select questions and activities that you will use.
- Have available newsprint, markers, paper, pens or pencils, and a map showing Paul's journeys (from a Bible or Bible atlas).
- If you plan to sing one of the hymns suggested for the Conclusion, arrange to have an accompanist and/or choir member lead the singing.
- What other questions, issues, or themes occur to you from your reflection?

Gathering

- Provide simple refreshments as people arrive and name tags if they are still needed.

Opening Worship

Prayer (unison)

Dear God, you are the source of all that is good. Open our hearts to the beauty all around and within so that we may rejoice with you in the goodness of your creation, even in times of danger and distress; through Jesus Christ our Lord. Amen.

Prayerful, Reflective Reading

- Read Philippians 4:4–7 aloud.
- Invite all to reflect for a few minutes in silence.
- After reflection time, invite all to listen for a word or phrase as the passage is read again and to reflect on that word or phrase in silence.
- Read the passage a third time, asking all to offer a silent prayer following the reading.
- Invite volunteers to share the word or phrase that spoke most deeply to them.

Prayer

Loving God, hear our prayers today as we seek to follow you more faithfully:

(*spoken prayers may be offered*)

Hear us now as we pray together, saying, Our Father . . .

Conversation

- Introduce chapter 2, "Great Joy." Share observations, reflections, and insights.
- Review the Introduction (pp. 7–8). Ask:

    How does it change your understanding of the Philippians 4 passage to know that Paul wrote it while in prison?

    Look on a map to see where Philippi is in relation to Ephesus and Rome, the possible places of Paul's imprisonment. Invite any participants who are familiar with letters written from prison by Dietrich Bonhoeffer or Martin Luther King Jr. to comment on similarities and differences between those writings and Paul's Letter to the Philippians. Invite participants to respond to question 1 in "For Reflection and Action" (p. 12).
- Review "A Basic Theme: 'Joyful, Joyful . . .'" (pp. 8–9). On a sheet of newsprint, write "joy" and "rejoice." Note that these and related words are used fourteen times in Philippians. Have someone read aloud Philippians 1:3–4 and 1:18b–19. Ask:

    What gives Paul joy?

Why does Paul rejoice even in the midst of suffering?

How can rejoicing be a spiritual discipline?

- Review "The Life of Faith: The Meaning of Joy" (pp. 9–10). Share these key points:
  a. Our modern tendency toward cynicism makes it hard to understand Paul's emphasis on joy.
  b. For Paul, joy points to the truth that God is sovereign, and therefore evil, suffering, and death will not have the last word.
  c. By rejoicing, we affirm our true destiny as creatures made in the image of God.
- Review "The Church: Rejoice . . . Always?" (pp. 10–12). Distribute paper and pens or pencils. Have participants reflect individually on how they might incorporate joy and gratitude into their lives as Christians. Suggest they start by considering questions 2 and 3 from "For Reflection and Action" (p. 12). Have them gather in groups of two or three and share their ideas.

Conclusion

- Read aloud together Philippians 4:4–7. Suggest that participants memorize the passage and reflect on it during their daily prayer time, as suggested in "Spiritual Practice" (p. 12).
- Sing one or more verses of a hymn of rejoicing, such as "Joyful, Joyful, We Adore Thee," "Rejoice, Ye Pure in Heart!," or "Rejoice, the Lord Is King!"[1]
- Close with the great benediction in Numbers 6:24, 26: "The LORD bless you and keep you; . . . the LORD lift up his countenance upon you, and give you peace."

Passing the Peace

The peace of Christ be with you.
    And also with you.
Amen.

---

1. This hymns can be found in many hymnals, including *Glory to God: Hymns, Psalms, and Spiritual Songs* (Louisville, KY: Westminster John Knox Press, 2013), 611, 804, and 363, respectively.

Beliefs That Matter

Main Idea

The hymn quoted in Philippians 2:5–11 reveals key aspects of Paul's theology: the weakness of the cross actually displays the power of God; what looks like a scandal and a stumbling block is, in fact, the means of our salvation; sacrificial love is at the heart of the divine character. To profess Christ as Lord means patterning one's life after Christ, who did not hold on to power but emptied himself and gave his life for the whole world.

Preparing to Lead

- Read and reflect on chapter 3, "Beliefs That Matter."
- Review this plan for the group gathering, and select questions and activities that you will use.
- Have available newsprint, markers, paper, and pens or pencils.
- If you plan to sing the hymn suggested for the Conclusion, arrange to have an accompanist and/or choir member lead the singing.
- What other questions, issues, or themes occur to you from your reflection?

Gathering

- Provide simple refreshments as people arrive and name tags if they are still needed.

Opening Worship

Prayer (unison)

Help us, dear God, to open our hearts and minds so that the mind of Christ will dwell in us, transform us, and draw us closer to one another and to you. Amen.

Prayerful, Reflective Reading

- Read Philippians 2:5–11 aloud.
- Invite all to reflect for a few minutes in silence.
- After reflection time, invite all to listen for a word or phrase as the passage is read again and to reflect on that word or phrase in silence.
- Read the passage a third time, asking all to offer a silent prayer following the reading.
- Invite volunteers to share the word or phrase that spoke most deeply to them.

Prayer

Loving God, hear our prayers today as we seek to follow you more faithfully:

(*spoken prayers may be offered*)

Hear us now as we pray together, saying, Our Father . . .

Conversation

- Introduce chapter 3, "Beliefs That Matter." Share observations, reflections, and insights.
- Review the Introduction (pp. 13–14). Note that Philippians 2:5–11 is thought to be a hymn that was used in worship by early Christians. Ask:

  What does this hymn tell us about Jesus?

  What are the "three movements" of the Jesus story as presented in the hymn? (coequal with God; self-emptying; exalted over all)

  What would have been controversial or subversive about the hymn at the time of Paul? Does any of it seem controversial today?

- Review "A Basic Theme: Theology in Poetry" (pp. 14–15). On a sheet of newsprint, write "Paul's Theology." Form several groups and give each group newsprint and markers. Have each group write at least three statements that express in their own words the theological claims made in this hymn. Suggest they read together any supporting Bible passages mentioned in the study book. Have someone from each group read the statements and post them for all to see.

- Review "The Life of Faith: Beliefs That Matter" (pp. 15–17). Call attention to the second paragraph about how Christian thought was influenced by Greek philosophy. Ask:

  How does the Philippians passage present a different way of thinking about God?

  Form several groups and discuss questions 1 and 2 in "For Reflection and Action" (p. 18). Have someone from each group report highlights of the discussion.

- Review "The Church: Whom Do We Worship?" (pp. 17–18). Have someone read aloud Philippians 2:9–11. On a sheet of newsprint, write "Christian exclusivism." Ask:

  What claims about Jesus in this passage might be labeled "exclusivist"?

  Do you find these claims easy or difficult to affirm?

  What does it mean to proclaim as Lord someone who "emptied himself" and became a servant?

  Form several small groups and discuss question 3 in "For Reflection and Action" (p. 18). Have someone from each group report on the discussion.

- Distribute paper and pens or pencils. Ask participants to reflect individually on who or what commands their highest allegiance by doing a "loyalty inventory," as suggested in "Spiritual Practice" (p. 18).

- Invite them to share their list with one or two others, if they are willing.

Conclusion

Sing together the hymn "At the Name of Jesus."[2]

2. This hymn can be found in many hymnals, including *Glory to God: Hymns, Psalms, and Spiritual Songs* (Louisville, KY: Westminster John Knox Press, 2013), 264.

Passing the Peace

The peace of Christ be with you.
    And also with you.
Amen.

Being of One Mind

Main Idea

In the face of conflict, Paul calls Christians to be "of one mind," to have "the mind of Christ." This does not mean merely intellectual agreement or social conformity but also being in community with people of different ethnicities, genders, and social and economic status, knowing that we all belong to God.

Preparing to Lead

- Read and reflect on chapter 4, "Being of One Mind."
- Review this plan for the group gathering, and select questions and activities that you will use.
- Have available newsprint, markers, paper, and pens or pencils.
- What other questions, issues, or themes occur to you from your reflection?

Gathering

- Provide simple refreshments as people arrive and name tags if they are still needed.

Opening Worship

Prayer (unison)

Dear God, you have made us to be members of one body in Jesus Christ. Open our hearts and minds to discover this new reality and to deepen the ties that bind us to one another and to Christ. Amen.

Prayerful, Reflective Reading
- Read Philippians 2:1–5, 12–17 aloud.
- Invite all to reflect for a few minutes in silence.
- After reflection time, invite all to listen for a word or phrase as the passage is read again and to reflect on that word or phrase in silence.
- Read the passage a third time, asking all to offer a silent prayer following the reading.
- Invite volunteers to share the word or phrase that spoke most deeply to them.

Prayer

Loving God, hear our prayers today as we seek to follow you more faithfully:

(*spoken prayers may be offered*)

Hear us now as we pray together, saying, Our Father . . .

Conversation
- Introduce chapter 4, "Being of One Mind." Share observations, reflections, and insights.
- Review the Introduction (pp. 19–20). On a sheet of newsprint, write "Conflict in the Church." Ask for a show of hands of those who (1) are surprised by the existence of conflict in the church or (2) have experienced conflict in church. Have participants form several groups and discuss question 1 in "For Reflection and Action" (p. 24). Have each group list on newsprint one or more issues that cause conflict in churches (doctrinal disagreements, money, worship styles, etc.). Post the lists for use later.
- Review "A Basic Theme: The Mind of Christ" (pp. 20–21). On a sheet of newsprint, write "being of one mind" and "the mind of Christ." Note that Paul says this is the key to resolving conflicts. Distribute paper and pens or pencils. Ask participants to jot down words and phrases that help them understand what Paul means by having "the mind of Christ" as someone reads aloud Philippians 2:1–4 from the NRSV and the translation by Bonnie Thurston (pp. 20–21). Invite them to share what they wrote. Ask:

Which translation of the passage do you prefer? Why?

What do verses 5–8 of the hymn Paul quotes suggest about "the mind of Christ"?

How does having "the mind of Christ" help prevent or resolve conflicts?

How might the language about considering others better than oneself be misused?

- Review "The Life of Faith: What Is the Nature of the Unity We Seek?" (pp. 21–23). Share these key points:
  a. In Philippians there seem to be two threats to the community: internal disagreements (such as the one between Euodia and Syntyche referenced in 4:2) and external persecution (the reason Paul is in prison).
  b. In urging unity, Paul does not seem to be emphasizing agreement about doctrines, or social conformity, but being "in Christ" in relationship with others who share the faith.
  c. Being "in Christ" means being in community with those who are different.
- Review "The Church: Unity, Diversity, and Community" (pp. 23–24). On a sheet of newsprint, write "Christianity is a religion of belonging." Ask:

    Do you agree that an overemphasis on individualism creates divisions among people today?

    What practices or insights does the church have to offer that might help overcome those divisions?

Form several groups and discuss questions 2 and 3 in "For Reflection and Action" (pp. 24–25). Have someone from each group report on the discussion. To practice seeking common ground with those who are different, have participants pair up and choose a topic from the lists made earlier of things that cause conflict in churches. Suggest they choose one on which they genuinely disagree or at least can role-play different points of view. Have them practice listening deeply to each other, as suggested in "Spiritual Practice" (p. 24). Invite each pair to share something they learned from the exercise.

Conclusion

Read aloud together Philippians 2:12–13 as a benediction.

Passing the Peace

The peace of Christ be with you.
  And also with you.
Amen.

Christian Identity

Main Idea

To be a Christian is to be transformed into a new person "in Christ." Instead of seeing right relationship with God as something to be attained, Paul came to see that it was a gift bestowed by God because of Christ's faithful obedience. God's gift makes it possible for us to strive to grow into the identity we have been given.

Preparing to Lead

- Read and reflect on chapter 5, "Christian Identity."
- Review this plan for the group gathering, and select questions and activities that you will use.
- Have available newsprint, markers, paper, and pens or pencils.
- What other questions, issues, or themes occur to you from your reflection?

Gathering

- Provide simple refreshments as people arrive and name tags if they are still needed.

Opening Worship

Prayer (unison)

O Christ, help us to see you more clearly, love you more dearly, and follow you more nearly, day by day. Amen.

Prayerful, Reflective Reading

- Read Philippians 3:7–14 aloud.
- Invite all to reflect for a few minutes in silence.

- After reflection time, invite all to listen for a word or phrase as the passage is read again and to reflect on that word or phrase in silence.
- Read the passage a third time, asking all to offer a silent prayer following the reading.
- Invite volunteers to share the word or phrase that spoke most deeply to them.

Prayer

Loving God, hear our prayers today as we seek to follow you more faithfully:

(spoken prayers may be offered)

Hear us now as we pray together, saying, Our Father . . .

Conversation

- Introduce chapter 5, "Christian Identity." Share observations, reflections, and insights. Have participants pair up and share their faith journeys using question 1 in "For Reflection and Action" (p. 31).
- Review the Introduction (pp. 27–28). On a sheet of newsprint, write "What does it mean to be a Christian?" Underneath, in two columns, invite participants to list things "Some Say" (i.e., obeying Jesus' teachings, believing Jesus is the Son of God) and things "Paul Says" (becoming a new person in Christ, trusting in Christ, living in right relationship with God, sharing in the life and suffering of Christ).
- Review "A Basic Theme: 'Living Is Christ' (1:21)" (pp. 28–29). Have someone read aloud Philippians 1:21. Form several groups and discuss what Paul means by "living is Christ." Have the groups share insights. Read aloud Philippians 3:8–9. Note the translation differences discussed on page 29. Have participants return to their groups and discuss question 3 in "For Reflection and Action" (p. 31). Have someone from each group report on the discussion. Ask:

    What things does Paul regard "as rubbish"? Why?

    What is Paul's relationship with the law of Moses?

    How does Paul understand his imprisonment and suffering?

- Review "The Life of Faith: 'Pressing On toward the Goal'" (pp. 29–30). Ask:

  How is running a race a good metaphor for the Christian life? (New life in Christ is a work in progress; it requires hard work.) What could be misleading about the race metaphor? (Discipleship is not a competition. New life in Christ is not something we earn by our own efforts; it is a gift from God.)

  What does Paul mean by to "attain the resurrection"?

  How can our new identity in Christ be both a gift and something we must strive for?

  Distribute paper and pens or pencils, and ask participants to reflect individually on question 2 in "For Reflection and Action" (p. 31). Invite them to write down ideas and share them with one or two others. Invite participants to add insights about "What does it mean to be a Christian?" to the list on newsprint begun earlier.

Conclusion

Suggest that participants select a spiritual discipline to engage in during the upcoming week, as suggested in "Spiritual Practice" (p. 30).

Read aloud together Philippians 3:20–4:1 as a benediction.

Passing the Peace

The peace of Christ be with you.
  And also with you.
Amen.

Mutual Hospitality

Main Idea

Hospitality is a relationship in which both parties are mutually transformed. Extending hospitality to the outsider is at the heart of biblical faith. Lydia's hospitality to Paul laid the foundation for the Philippian church and its exemplary spiritual practices of hospitality and generosity.

Preparing to Lead

- Read and reflect on chapter 6, "Mutual Hospitality."
- Review this plan for the group gathering, and select questions and activities that you will use.
- Have available newsprint and markers.
- What other questions, issues, or themes occur to you from your reflection?

Gathering

- Provide simple refreshments as people arrive and name tags if they are still needed.

Opening Worship

Prayer (unison)

Dear God, as you opened Lydia's heart to receive the good news, open our eyes to see you in all we meet. Amen.

Prayerful, Reflective Reading

- Read Acts 16:11–15 aloud.
- Invite all to reflect for a few minutes in silence.

58

- After reflection time, invite all to listen for a word or phrase as the passage is read again and to reflect on that word or phrase in silence.
- Read the passage a third time, asking all to offer a silent prayer following the reading.
- Invite volunteers to share the word or phrase that spoke most deeply to them.

Prayer

Loving God, hear our prayers today as we seek to follow you more faithfully:

(*spoken prayers may be offered*)

Hear us now as we pray together, saying, Our Father . . .

Conversation

- Introduce chapter 6, "Mutual Hospitality." Share observations, reflections, and insights.
- Review the Introduction (pp. 33–34). On a sheet of newsprint, write "Who was Lydia?" Invite participants to call out things that Acts 16:11–15 and the study book (pp. 33–34) tell us about Lydia. List these on the newsprint. Be sure to include actions as well as attributes.
- Review "A Basic Theme: Hospitality, a Two-Way Street" (pp. 34–35). On a sheet of newsprint, write "Mutual Hospitality." Draw an arrow pointing left and under it an arrow pointing right, to illustrate a two-way street. At one end of the arrows, write "giver," and at the other end, write "recipient." Ask:

  Who were the givers in the Philippians story? How and what did they give?

  Who were the recipients? What did they receive?

List on the newsprint Paul, Lydia, Epaphroditus, and the Philippian church, noting that all of them both gave and received. Divide into several groups and discuss:

How are you a giver and a recipient in your congregation?

What gifts do new members bring and receive? (See question 1 in "For Reflection and Action," p. 38.)

Have someone from each group report highlights of the discussion.

• Review "The Life of Faith: The 'Disciplined' Life" (pp. 35–37). On a sheet of newsprint, write "Spiritual Disciplines/Practices." Invite participants to call out words or phrases that these terms bring to mind. List responses on the newsprint. Ask:

Why have Protestants, until recently, tended not to stress spiritual disciplines?

How can spiritual practices be helpful in the Christian life?

What two spiritual disciplines stand out in the Philippian community?

Write the answer (generosity and hospitality) on the newsprint if it is not already listed. Divide into groups and discuss question 2 in "For Reflection and Action" (p. 38), noting how Paul describes the generosity of the Philippians in 4:15–16. Have someone from each group report on the discussion.

• Review "The Church: Shaping a Hospitable World" (pp. 37–38). Share these key points:

a. The most revolutionary result of proclaiming the gospel was the creation of a new community where all were welcome.

b. Extending hospitality to the outsider is at the heart of biblical faith, from the law of Moses to the ministry of Jesus to the teachings of Paul.

Ask:

How can we (as individuals and as a congregation) show hospitality?

How do churches, cities, and nations today struggle with what it means to be hospitable (for example, with regard to immigration or low-income housing)?

Divide into several groups and discuss question 3 in "For Reflection and Action" (p. 38). Have someone from each group report on the discussion. Looking back over the study, invite any who are willing to share one thing they have learned from Philippians that will enrich their lives as followers of Christ.

Conclusion

Encourage participants to commit to showing hospitality in their interactions with others, as suggested in "Spiritual Practice" (p. 38).

Read aloud together Philippians 4:19–20 as a benediction.

Passing the Peace

The peace of Christ be with you.
    And also with you.
Amen.

Want to Know More?

Craddock, Fred B. *Philippians*. Interpretation: A Bible Commentary for Teaching and Preaching. Atlanta: John Knox Press, 1985. Paperback edition, Louisville, KY: Westminster John Knox Press, 2012. This is an older commentary, but it is well researched and very accessible to a wide audience.

Migliore, Daniel L. *Philippians and Philemon*. Belief: A Theological Commentary on the Bible. Louisville, KY: Westminster John Knox Press, 2014. A more recent study, it focuses on theological themes and contemporary parallels.

Thurston, Bonnie B., and Judith M. Ryan. *Philippians and Philemon*. Sacra Pagina 10. Collegeville, MN: Liturgical Press, 2005. This is by far the most technical commentary, but it also has the most extensive discussion of the background and context of Paul's writing.

CPSIA information can be obtained
at www.ICGtesting.com
Printed in the USA
JSHW040815240920
8188JS00007B/98